Contents

Title page: Bronze-winged Parrot, *Pionus chalcopterus*. Photo by Harry V. Lacey.

Photographs: G. Allen, 30 top. All-Pets Photo, 17. Archiv Klinik fuer Gefluegel TiHo Hannover, 47 bottom. L. Arnall, 43 46 top. G. Axelrod, 27 bottom, 42 bottom, 57 top. H. R. Axelrod, 6 bottom, 8 bottom, 19, 27 top, 28, 29, 34 top, 35, 42 top, 48, 50, 51, 52, 53 bottom, 54 top, 56, 58 bottom, 65, 68, 69. C. Bickford, 9. E. W. Burr, 46 bottom. R. Cathcart, 34 bottom, J. Daniel, 47 top. M. Guevara, 66. R. Hanson, 22. M. Heidenreich, 45 bottom. I. Huff, 24 bottom. N. Kummerfeld, 44 top, 45 top, H.V. Lacey, 12, 20, 33, 39, 41, 63. P. Leyson, 13, 59. A. J. Mobbs, 7, 16, 18. J. Moore, 54 bottom. E. J. Mulawka, 36. F. Nothaft, 38. F. Prenzel, 10. L. Robinson, 14, 15, 61 top, 62 top. Courtesy of San Diego Zoo, 25, 40 top, 60. W. C. Satterfield, 70, 71, 72, 73, 74, 75, 76, 77. H. Schultz, 53 top. V. Serbin, 23, 31, 32, 55. T. Silva, 21, 24 top, 44 bottom. R. Small, 40 bottom. Courtesy of Vogelpark Walsrode, 6 top, 8 top, 11, 58 top, 61 bottom, 62 bottom, 64. M. M. Vriends, 57 bottom.

© **1982 T.F.H. Publications, Inc., Ltd.**

ISBN 0-87666-806-6

Distributed in the U.S. by T.F.H. Publications, Inc., 211 West Sylvania Avenue, PO Box 427, Neptune, NJ 07753; in England by T.F.H. (Gt. Britain) Ltd., 13 Nutley Lane, Reigate, Surrey; in Canada to the pet trade by Rolf C. Hagen Ltd., 3225 Sartelon Street, Montreal 382, Quebec; in Canada to the book trade by H & L Pet Supplies, Inc., 27 Kingston Crescent, Kitchener, Ontario N28 2T6; in Southeast Asia by Y.W. Ong, 9 Lorong 36 Geylang, Singapore 14; in Australia and the South Pacific by Pet Imports Pty. Ltd., P.O. Box 149, Brookvale 2100, N.S.W. Australia; in South Africa by Valid Agencies, P.O. Box 51901, Randburg 2125 South Africa. Published by T.F.H. Publications, Inc., Ltd., the British Crown Colony of Hong Kong.

The T.F.H. Book of
PARROTS

Edited by W.A. STARIKA and E.L. RICHARDSON

Parrot Lore

No one can say how long parrots have been kept as pets, since their association with man goes back before the time of recorded history. As pets, it is likely they are as ancient as domestic cats and dogs. Strong evidence for the great antiquity of parrots in captivity is found by anyone who has visited primitive people throughout the tropical world. Primitive Indians of South America will tell you that they have always caught and tamed parrots. The same story is told by natives in Africa, Australia and Asia. As long as the human species has been intelligent enough to crave the companionship of animals, man has been keeping company with parrots.

Parrots probably were introduced to the western world by the ancient Greeks and Romans, whose conquests extended into Africa and Asia Minor, where certain parrot species occur in the wild. Alexander the Great had pet parrots three hundred years before the birth of Christ. He is believed to have given tamed parrots from India to Aristotle, who mentions them in his writings.

The Romans kept both Asian and African parrots. Emperors and wealthy citizens had them in their homes and even established aviaries for them. Pet parrots became so much the rage in ancient Rome that a lively import business was established.

In Europe two important developments gave impetus to parrot keeping: heated homes and the great explorers who circled the globe in the fifteenth and sixteenth centuries. First the sailors brought back the parrots of Africa and Asia and later those of America and Australia.

Christopher Columbus and his men brought back tales of brilliantly colored birds in the New World. Within a few years sailors were buying or stealing tame parrots from the natives of the Caribbean Islands, South America and Central America. Within a century after Columbus's voyages to the New World, parrots had gained great popularity throughout Western Europe.

Writers of stories about sailing ships and pirates always included a parrot or two. Familiar parrot quotations like Stevenson's "Pieces of Eight! Pieces of Eight!" still arouse visions of the high seas and one-eyed, peg-legged pirates. The association of parrots with buccaneers is so close that even today the sight of a brilliantly colored specimen is likely to stimulate pictures in the mind's eye of square-rigged ships and pirate treasures.

Ring-necked parakeets were certainly known to ancient Greece. Today, the Rose-ringed Parakeet, *Psittacula krameri*, is the most familiar; the wild coloration appears below, the lutino variety above.

While the New World has provided many of the parrots most popular in aviculture, other neotropical species are not well known. Among these is the Bronze-winged Parrot, *Pionus chalcopterus*.

What Is a Parrot?

Parrots all belong to the family Psittacidae, of which there are more than 300 species occurring throughout the world's tropical and semi-tropical belt. They are generally very active, gregarious, strong-flying birds. To those who have seen them only in cages or chained to perches, this will come as a surprise. Anyone who has travelled in tropical rain forests, however, knows them for their raucous chattering in tall trees and for their strong, erratic flight.

Parrots have distinctive features that make them easily recognizable. They have large heads and powerful curved beaks, the upper portion extending down over the lower. The upper portion is hinged and movable; this distinguishes parrots from hook-billed birds like the hawks and owls. The upper portion of a raptor's bill is fixed to the bony structure of the skull. The smallest parrots can bite hard enough to hurt. The larger ones can inflict a severe wound and may even break small bones. For this reason a strange bird should always be approached with caution. Parrot tongues are fat and rough, ideally adapted for shelling the nuts and crushing the fruits that form the bulk of their diet in the wild state.

The toes of parrots are made for grasping, and the short, stocky legs are suited to climbing. The two middle toes point forward and the two outer ones extend backward. A long, sharp claw extends from each. Many parrots are brilliantly colored, with nearly every color imaginable represented in the family.

Most species have a loud, harsh call that is capable of much variation. This, combined with a high level of intelligence, gives them their remarkable ability to imitate human speech.

In nature most parrots nest in hollow trees. The abandoned hollows of woodpeckers are often used. Most parrots are faithful mates, and in many species both parents care for the eggs and young. Newly hatched parrots are usually naked and quite helpless. They develop slowly, growing on regurgitated food provided by the parents.

The larger parrots are capable of living for a long time. For this reason a young parrot is a good investment. There are plenty of authentic records of parrots living for over fifty years.

As mentioned earlier, parrots are found throughout the tropical world. One species, the extinct Carolina Parakeet, occasionally travelled as far north as Canada in the sum-

These species all exhibit the characteristic features of the parrot family—White-headed Parrot, *Pionus seniloides* (above); Red-winged Parrot, *Aprosmictus erythropterus* (below); and the Red-bellied Macaw, *Ara manilata* (facing page).

The Crimson Rosella, *Platycercus elegans*, from Australia is a good example of the brilliant, contrasting coloration exhibited by many parrots.

mer. But how did the parrot family become so widely distributed? Of course, the answer lies in their gift of powerful flight. Biologists and paleontologists believe that they once lived in the northern portions of the world during times when these latitudes had mild climates. (Fossil parrots found in Europe and North America bear this out.) As the northern climate become cooler, the parrots were forced to fly ever closer to the equator. As the seas shifted many birds became isolated. In their isolation, they developed many distinctive features, but they remained similar in important ways.

In summary, a parrot is a brightly colored tropical bird with a strong beak, a large brain, grasping claws and powerful wings.

Parrots are often divided into two groups: Old World Parrots and New World Parrots. This classification, however, has some serious shortcomings. For instance, to which group do the parrots of Australia and the South Seas belong? For the hobbyist, it makes a lot more sense to group them according to size: large parrots and small parrots.

Two large parrots: the Blue-fronted Amazon, *Amazona aestiva* (above) and the Eclectus Parrot, *Eclectus roratus* (below, a hen) are both around fourteen inches in length, from bill to tail.

THE LARGE PARROTS

Everyone who has ever visited the aviary of a zoo will remember the huge, brilliantly colored macaws of South and Central America. As pets, the macaws should be kept only by those in a position to care for them. They need lots of room because of their great size (up to forty inches tip-to-tip). Their loud, raucous calls are apt to irritate human ears, and they tend to be hostile toward strangers. With their large, powerful beaks they can inflict a painful wound. They are not usually good talkers, although there are exceptions. On the other hand, macaws are extremely intelligent and properly handled can be taught many tricks. Macaws are best kept by those with experience and the space to keep them happy.

The amazons (of which there are twenty-seven species all belonging to the genus *Amazona*) are the most desirable of the New World parrots. They occur throughout South America, Central America and the Caribbean Islands. Amazons become good talkers and appealing pets.

If they are constantly annoyed, they can develop the obnoxious habit of screaming, but knowing this, owners of amazons should protect them from children and childish adults. At least a half-dozen species of amazons are commonly sold in the United States.

The African Grey Parrot at one time was the most popular of the larger birds. It is probably the best talker of the entire family. Most of those put up for sale are older birds. If you are considering buying one, you should be aware of this possibility. The eye of a baby African Grey is dark. As it matures the iris lightens, as do the patches of skin around the eyes.

Cockatoos are birds of great beauty, both in color and in form. Unfortunately they are also scarce in the United States. They come from Australia and neighboring islands, and there are strict laws banning their exportation. If you are fortunate enough to acquire one of the five or so species occasionally sold, you will have a fine pet, because their beauty is matched by their pleasant disposition.

Eclectus Parrots are native to Australia and several islands in the South Pacific. These brilliantly marked birds have feathers which resemble finely combed fur. Males and females are entirely different in color, and because of this, the two sexes were at one time considered two different species by ornithologists. These birds can learn to talk and will breed in captivity, but unfortunately there are not many in the United States.

THE SMALL PARROTS

Because of their compactness, many of the smaller parrots have gained great popularity as house pets. Everyone is

A shipment of Sun Conures, *Aratinga solstitialis*.

familiar with the appealing little Budgerigar, or budgie. Generally speaking, the small parrots are not so good at talking as the large ones.

Cockatiels are twelve-inch birds from Australia. They are gentle and adapt well to captivity.

Lovebirds are short (about six inches), stocky birds from Africa. Most of them are predominantly green, although many have brilliant patches of color. They make amusing pets, but they can be trained to talk only with difficulty.

Several little parrots of the genus *Brotogeris* make colorful, friendly pets. Most come from Central America and northern South America, but some are found in other parts of that continent. The best known of this group is the attractive Orange-chinned Parakeet, which in several subspecies has a rather wide distribution.

The conures, from South America, bear a strong physical resemblance to the macaws, to which they are closely related. Like most other small parrots, the conures are likely to be poor talkers, but they are hardy and friendly.

The very colorful rosellas are native to Australia. They are usually regarded more as aviary birds than as pets.

Caiques are two species of small parrots from South America. They are intelligent, amusing birds and make very interesting pets.

Lories and lorikeets, from Australasia, can be tamed and can make good pets, but since they are very active birds, they would probably do better in an aviary than in a cage.

Other popular parrots include members of the genus *Psittacula*—found mostly in Asia—and the genera *Psephotus, Polytelis* and *Neophema*—all from Australia.

Many fanciers hold the opinion that Fischer's Lovebird, *Agapornis fischeri*, is the most beautiful of the genus.

Why Keep Parrots?

There are thousands of colorful, appealing birds throughout the world that would make nice pets—if they could be domesticated. If you have ever attempted to keep any of our common wild birds, you know that most of them just don't adapt to confinement. It is a distressing experience to watch a songbird dash itself to death in a cage or collapse and die of fright before your eyes.

This is not true of parrots; they adapt readily to captivity even when captured as adults, and they frequently develop a strong attachment to their owner. Apparently something in their well-developed brain helps them to adjust to strange conditions.

Still, there are plenty of other birds that can be domesticated, but parrots possess special attributes that place them at the very top as pet birds.

Nearly everyone associates parrots with the ability to talk. This is what sets them apart from other colorful birds. Compare a parrot's head with its body and then make a similar comparison with other birds. You will find that the parrots have very large heads for the body size. The large, well-developed brain provides them with the intelligence to imitate the human voice and to learn delightful tricks.

Color is another important attribute of parrots. Pick a color—any color—and somewhere in the world there is a member of the parrot family sporting that color in its plumage.

Once adjusted to their owners, parrots are friendly birds. Often they develop a warm devotion to their masters. By the same token, some parrots have an uncanny knack for sensing the people who don't like them. They respond to their enemies with loud cries, uneasiness and even aggressiveness.

Parrots are easy to care for. Give them the warmth of an average home, pleasant surroundings, clean living quarters, the simple foods they require, and all they ask in addition is love and affection. Few pets require so little for the satisfaction and pleasure they so generously give.

Some kinds of parrots can be induced to breed in captivity. The odd, helpless babies, tenderly cared for by their affectionate parents, add a delightful dimension to keeping birds.

The coloration of parrots varies from the bold to the subtle. These species are both native to Australia: the Princess Parrot, *Polytelis alexandrae* (above) and the Australian King Parrot, *Alisterus scapularis* (facing page).

14

Many amazon species native to Caribbean Islands are endangered; for example, the populations of most of the subspecies of the Cuban Amazon, *Amazona leucocephala*, are very small.

Perhaps the most famous parrot is the African Grey, *Psittacus erithacus*; however, the records for longevity appear to be held by the amazons.

Longevity is a priceless quality of parrots. How sad it is to own a pet that lives only long enough for its owner to develop a strong attachment to it—not so with parrots. It is claimed that some of the larger species have lived for eighty years! There are many authenticated records of parrots living for thirty years or more. Even the tiny budgie will live for ten to twenty years if it is well cared for.

Add up the attributes: ability to talk, color, friendliness, devotion to their owners, ease of care, willingness to breed, long life. And just to place the cherry on the sundae, add the parrot's long, romantic history—pirates and sailing vessels and Roman conquerors—to the list. What other pets have so much to offer?

Selecting a Parrot

The Purple-bellied Parrot, *Triclaria malachitacea*, is a good example of a parrot that appears relatively common in its range, yet has been little studied in the wild and has rarely been available to aviculturists.

Four factors are important in deciding which particular parrot is the right one for you: appeal to you personally, health, age and previous training.

The matter of appeal is entirely an individual thing. The bird of the color, size and disposition to suit you may not appeal to another person at all. Hence, only you can decide the aesthetic aspect of parrot purchasing. Aesthetics, however, should be tempered by other factors mentioned elsewhere in this book. For instance, if you live in a one-room city apartment, you must consider carefully before deciding about a large, beautiful Scarlet Macaw regardless of how much it appeals to you personally.

Choosing a healthy bird is not always a simple matter. By far the most important factor is choosing a pet dealer with a good reputation. A reputable dealer will not put a sick bird up for sale at any price. The price of a bird is another factor to watch. If the bargain price is too low, you have a right to be suspicious. A bargain bird may be a genuine bargain, but it may also be a bird which the dealer for some reason wants to get rid of. Look all cheap birds over carefully and quiz the dealer about them.

There are a few clues to good health that anyone can look for. The eyes of healthy birds are bright and clear. There should be no growths on the horny area of the beak or elsewhere. Breathing should be quiet and steady. Noisy, irregular breathing may indicate some lung or respiratory disease. Notice bare areas where there should be feathers. The bird should be sleek and tight-feathered. A bird that spends much of its time with its feathers fluffed up may be sick. The droppings should be well formed and not watery.

Most people feel that they are making a better investment if they choose a young bird. There *is* considerable merit to buying a young bird, but this factor alone should not keep you from buying one that appeals to you. Remember, a ten-year-old may live for another thirty years! Heavy scales on the legs and/or rough eye rings indicate older birds. A reputable dealer will tell you how old a parrot is, if he knows.

Previous training of a parrot may be worth quite a lot to you, for it can save you much time. A bird with some training

This young Lutino Cockatiel, *Nymphicus hollandicus*, exhibits all the characteristics of a healthy bird.

Recently imported Nanday Conures, *Nandayus nenday*, characteristically move to the farthest corner of the cage when approached.

The steady gaze shows that this Scaly-headed Parrot, *Pionus maximiliani*, is obviously accustomed to human presence.

will not become excessively excited when a person approaches the cage. To see if a parrot is hand-trained, insert your hand into the cage very slowly, palm down. Move the side of your hand to the bird's toes. If the parrot accepts this approach calmly, it probably has been hand-trained. While approaching a parrot with your hand, however, keep an eye on its bill, for it may bite. If a bird shows no indication of being hand-trained, you should not reject it if it appeals to you otherwise, because with some patience you can do the training. But watch out for any parrot that rears back and screeches when your hand approaches. Dealers call such birds "broncos." A bronco is an excessively wild bird or one that may have been mistreated. To overcome the bad disposition of a bronco may require more patience than you possess.

If you have several similar parrots to choose from, as a general rule you should pick the one that shows the fewest signs of nervousness. This is the one that will probably respond best to training. The one that flies in panic at the first sight of your hand should be avoided.

Parrot Care

The first consideration in the care of a parrot is *kindness*. No animal can be expected to become a devoted pet if it is mistreated. Parrots, especially, are quick to sense the love of an owner, and they respond to it. Children (and some adults) must be instructed never to scare or tease them. Incidentally, this is an important additional reason for bringing any pet into a household: to teach children kindness. Parrots should never be punished. Although they are intelligent, they are not bright enough to know why they are being punished. In days fortunately gone by, parrots being trained were often rapped on the head when they failed to respond to instructions. The result invariably was a noisy, nasty or terrified bird. In everything done to and for a parrot, kindness must be kept in mind.

Like most pets, parrots are inclined to be messy. They scatter seed about. They splash in their water. Their droppings are apt to spread beyond the confines of their cage. They chew anything they can get their beaks into and toss the pieces around. If you aren't prepared to spend some time in housekeeping, you shouldn't consider keeping a parrot.

HOUSING

Parrots are kept in a variety of ways. They can be chained to a perch, but this may create too much mess for some people to tolerate, and many people don't like the idea of chains. It is too reminiscent of chain gangs and galley slaves.

Cages make the most satisfactory homes in most situations. They should be large enough to allow the bird to move about without difficulty. The bird's tail should not be constantly rubbing against the sides of the cage, and it should be able to spread its wings to the full. Square cages are best. The cage should be provided with two or more stout wooden perches placed near the center. Water and food containers should be changeable from the outside. The bottom of the cage should be removable for cleaning.

The cage should be constructed of metal since wooden cages are quickly chewed to pieces. It should be located in a bright place away from drafts. In front of windows is fine if the windows are well sealed and weather stripped. If the location is sunny, cover part of the front of the cage to prevent overheating and, possibly, sunstroke.

For the serious hobbyist with several parrots, an aviary is the ideal enclosure. A well-designed aviary provides parrots

Both the sulphur-crested cockatoo in the cage and the Galah, *Eolophus roseicapillus*, atop it enjoy some time beside a bright window. While sturdy metal cages may be the most suitable enclosures for the larger parrots, the birds' needs for activity may not be met; therefore, owners should allow for supervised time outside the cage. The open door encourages the Blue-fronted Amazon, *Amazona aestiva* (facing page) to climb out.

with room for exercise, flight and nesting. In mild climates, the aviary may be built outdoors.

Aviaries must be of sturdy construction, since parrots are strong and active. If the aviary is outdoors it must be built to keep out the neighbor's cat and wild predators. The design of the aviary is a matter of individual taste, but the construction is of some importance. The most durable ones are built entirely of metal, perhaps with a pipe frame supporting wire mesh. If the frame is wooden, the wood must be covered with wire mesh to reduce damage from the parrot's chewing.

Size of the aviary is a matter of taste, available space and cost. If it is outdoors, it should be located where the birds can bask in the sun if they wish, but it should provide shade as well. Several wooden perches should be located around the enclosure.

Whether or not breeding is desired, an aviary should have nest boxes, with holes just large enough for entry. The number of boxes required will depend upon the number of birds in the aviary. If the box is made of wood it will eventually be chewed up. Many owners use small galvanized garbage pails with a hole cut in the side. Regardless of what is used, the box should have a removable top for cleaning and inspection. The nest box should be several feet off the floor, perhaps fastened to the side of the aviary.

The aviary must be shielded against wind. Some are built against buildings for shelter, and others are built with one or more solid sides.

Aviaries must be constructed of sturdy wire, both for smaller species like the Monk Parakeet, *Myiopsitta monachus* (above) or for amazons like the Green-cheeked, *Amazona viridigenalis* (below).

The floor of the aviary (if it is outdoors) may be dirt or concrete. Concrete is most satisfactory because it can be swept and hosed. Indoors, the floor of the aviary must be sufficiently waterproof to withstand frequent scrubbing.

All parrots are adapted to tropical or subtropical climates. Hence, they cannot endure extreme cold. Parrots kept outdoors in the summer or in the southern parts of the United States can endure fairly cold temperatures if they have lots of room to move about. However, parrots kept in small cages, indoors or out, quickly succumb when the temperature falls. If the temperature of your house drops at night, the cage should be covered. If it is necessary to take a parrot outdoors in the winter, the cage should be carefully covered and brought back indoors as quickly as possible.

Parrots respond positively to bright light. In the sun's rays they are active and talkative. In dim light they just sit. Of course the direct summer sun may be too hot for a heavily feathered bird, so shade should be provided over part of the area.

Perches used in a cage or an aviary are of considerable importance, as the parrot spends nearly all of its time grasping

As all parrots are native to warmer climates, only in such regions can they be kept outdoors, the year around. The cockatoo here is Major Mitchell's, *Cacatua leadbeateri.*

The tree branch here is a good size for the grip of the
African Grey, *Psittacus erithacus*.

For bathing, most parrots prefer shallow vessels. The "Shamrock" Macaw is a cross between a Military and a Scarlet.

On many cages designed for parrots the wiring is horizontal to facilitate climbing and the door swings down so that the bird can move in and out easily, as this Jandaya Conure, *Aratinga jandaya*, does.

one. The larger the bird, the larger the diameter of the perch required. While a lovebird may be content with a three-eighths-inch perch, a large parrot would soon tire of grasping such a spindling. The largest parrots need perches the diameter of a broom handle. Ideally, the perch should be oval rather than round.

CLEANING

Cleanliness is said to be next to godliness. It is more than that. Cleanliness is also healthful. A parrot that is kept in a dirty cage is much more likely to contract a disease than one kept in clean surroundings. Also, a parrot maintained in a clean cage is much more appealing aesthetically since the odor from a dirty cage can permeate the entire house. Parrots enjoy taking a bath once in a while. They can be placed out in a warm summer rain or they will enjoy standing under a lukewarm shower.

Parrots should be kept away from other birds because some bird diseases are contagious. If a parrot is kept outdoors in the summer, care should be exercised to see that wild birds don't visit the cage for food. A wild bird may carry disease.

Some chores must be done daily if a parrot is to remain in the best of health. Water must be changed every day. Food should be checked periodically. If the food is fresh fruit or greens, it should not be allowed to rot. The floor of the cage must be cleaned several times a week. About once a week remove the parrot from its cage and give the cage a scrubbing with hot soapy water, and then thoroughly rinse it and dry it before placing the parrot back in its cage.

FEEDING EQUIPMENT

Most cages come with food and water containers that can be serviced from the outside. These are best, but almost any small container can be used to hold food. If it is fairly high, a container should have an edge that permits the bird to stand on it. Containers so large as to permit the bird to stand in them are not desirable. With a large container a parrot will scatter seed and will mix its own waste with the food. Pet shops sell many cleverly designed feeders.

Feeding

It is not well known that even seedeating parrots like the Peach-faced Lovebird, *Agapornis roseicollis* (above) will be healthier if fruits and vegetables are offered. Of course, these foods are the main constituents of the diet for lories (facing page).

The parrot's natural diet would likely be unsuitable for pet parrots. Wild parrots eat large quantities of nuts, palm nuts and seeds of trees and fruits. All of these are rich in high-calorie substances, especially fats. For wild parrots such a diet is ideal because their very active habits demand a great many calories. Caged parrots, however, lead a very sedentary life. Just as a man who works at a desk requires fewer calories than a man who does hard physical labor, so a caged parrot needs fewer calories than a wild parrot.

The diet of pet parrots should be high in protein and bulk. Caged parrots will continue to eat all of the high-calorie foods by preference if they are permitted to do so, but their health will be damaged if they become too fat. Fortunately or otherwise, a pet parrot must eat whatever its owner gives it. Thus it is possible to provide a more wholesome diet. If a pet parrot suffers from malnutrition, the owner alone is to blame.

One of the most commonly used parrot foods is sunflower seed. If permitted to do so, parrots will eat them almost to the exclusion of everything else. Unfortunately, sunflower seeds are very rich in fats. An experienced veterinarian can detect a parrot fed exclusively on sunflower seeds nearly every time. Such a bird will be fat, will have overgrown beak and claws, poor plumage, and there will be signs of mineral and vitamin deficiences. It may take some effort to wean a parrot that has been fed only sunflower seeds to other foods, but these seeds should be fed only as an occasional treat.

Chick-starter feed or laying mash is good for parrots, if they will eat it. Some refuse chick-starter altogether, but many will accept it after a period of conditioning.

Cuttlebone or ground oyster shell should be provided for calcium.

Corn, wheat, millet and canary seed are excellent foods, but the larger parrots will sometimes refuse to eat the smaller seeds. Rape seeds, hemp seeds, flax seeds and peanuts in too great a quantity may make caged parrots fat.

Many parrots will eat a wide variety of fruits, which are good for them. Bananas, especially, are enjoyed by parrots. Fruits should be fed sparingly at first because they may cause diarrhea until the bird's system becomes accustomed to them.

Greens should be fed regularly. Any of the dark green leafy greens like spinach, watercress, parsley, wild mustard,

The kind of seed eaten depends largely on the size of the species. The Cockatiel (left) takes small seeds like millet and also cracks sunflower, as do macaws. The Scarlet and Blue-and-Gold Macaws below are occupied shelling peanuts.

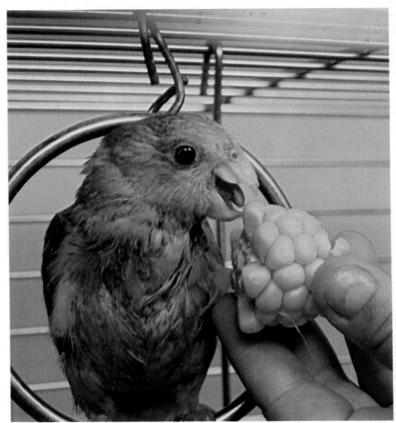

Feeding by hand is one of the most important taming procedures. Kernels of corn are relished by many birds, such as this immature Plum-headed Parakeet, *Psittacula cyanocephala*.

chickweed, beet greens, peas and carrot tops are good. The lighter green vegetables like lettuce and celery leaves are of less value because they contain fewer vitamins and minerals. Greens, like fruits, may cause diarrhea.

Nuts in their shells may be given as an occasional treat.

All seed-eating birds must have gravel because birds have no teeth with which to chew their food. Mixed with the hard seeds in the bird's gizzard, gravel helps to grind the seeds up. Don't use gravel from roads or driveways as it may contain tar, plant poison, insecticides and other harmful substances. Limestone and shells alone are unsatisfactory because they dissolve too readily. Usually it is best to purchase bird gravel from the pet store, since such gravel is prepared especially for birds.

Unless the parrot is fed one of the chick mixes, cod-liver oil (a rich source of vitamin D) should be added to the diet regularly. Cod-liver oil may be mixed with seeds in the amount of one teaspoonful per pound of seed, or a few drops may be placed on a small piece of bread.

Both cod-liver oil and feed mixed with cod-liver oil should be stored in the refrigerator in tightly sealed containers, since cod-liver oil turns rancid when exposed to air at room temperature.

It is important to establish a regular feeding schedule for parrots. Haphazard feeding is likely to lead to an unbalanced diet.

Training

Without training, a parrot is of little more value to a home than a decorative vase or a colorful painting. With training, a parrot can become a never-ending source of pleasure. Thus every parrot should be tamed, at the very least, to the extent of being willing to perch on one's finger. At best they can be trained to do delightful tricks, and many species can be taught to imitate human words.

Training a parrot takes a lot of patience and an attitude of affection. Young birds, from two to six months old, are the most easily trained, but even fairly old birds can learn. It just takes more patience. Even a nasty or mistreated parrot can be trained if one has patience.

The first step in training is to gain the parrot's confidence. Place the bird's cage in an area where much of the family activity takes place, such as near the television set in the living room. Sudden movements and harsh, loud noises should be avoided as these frighten a new bird. The owner should approach the cage frequently but slowly and talk to the parrot in a normal voice. In a surprisingly short time the bird will become completely accustomed to human activity.

Once the parrot has become accustomed to humans, confidence and affection can be increased by offering pieces of fruit like a banana or a grape, nuts, sunflower seeds and other tidbits held in one's fingers.

The next step in taming is to stick-train the parrot. Assuming the bird has learned to accept morsels from human hands, a stick (which for larger parrots can be as thick as a broom handle) is slowly placed under the breast and gentle pressure is exerted. Chances are, the bird will transfer its grip on the perch to the stick. If it doesn't respond at first, keep trying. If it becomes annoyed, discontinue efforts until another time. Once the parrot is accustomed to stepping up on the stick, the hand can be substituted. In taming a parrot, especially the larger ones, a heavy glove should be worn at first as the bird may bite, or it may grasp too tightly with its claws.

Don't try to take the hand-trained bird out of the cage at first. Wait until it has become thoroughly accustomed to hand-sitting in the cage, because a parrot associates its cage with security.

Removing the bird from the cage before it has become completely hand-trained may frighten it and undo what you already have accomplished. Before a hand-trained parrot is removed from the cage it is wise to have the flight feathers

Once the parrot has become accustomed to perching on your hand in the cage, the next step is to bring it out, still on your hand. These are immature Plum-headed Parakeets.

Budgerigars, *Melopsittacus undulatus*, are undoubtedly the most familiar of all the parrots. They are tamable and trainable, and some will learn to talk. Besides these characteristics, the many color varieties available, such as this pied light green, ensure their continued popularity.

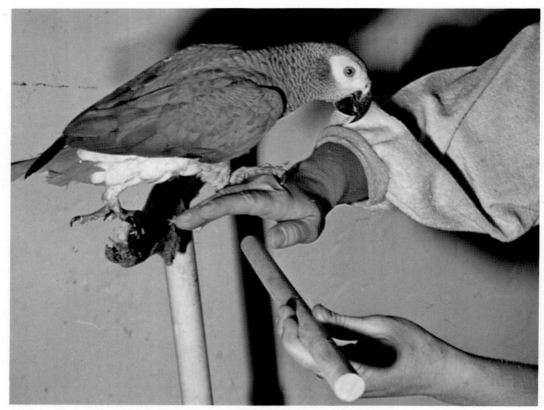

This African Grey has become used to stepping on and off a stick. Next, hand-training is practiced in the same way.

Macaws excel in performing tricks. This bicycle rider is a Scarlet Macaw, *Ara macao*.

The amount of feather clipping—and whether to clip just one wing or both—depends on how strong a flier the bird is and what you intend to accomplish. On this Nanday Conure wing, only a few feathers have been cut, in order to retard the bird's flight. The two outermost feathers are often left intact to preserve appearance.

clipped by your pet dealer or a veterinarian. Done properly, clipping the wings is painless, and it prevents the parrot from flying away. If a parrot that is not wing-clipped flies away, it is likely to be a thoroughly terrified bird by the time it is caught and returned to its cage. It may even be injured. Clipping is a good precaution against undoing many weeks of gaining your pet's confidence.

If the parrot should get loose in the house before it is completely tame, don't chase it. Walk towards it, talking to it in a soothing voice. Extend your hand and attempt to get the bird to sit on it. If the bird is too frightened to respond, it may be necessary to be more resourceful. If the cage is brought close, the bird may walk in. If not, drop a light cloth over the bird and pick it up enveloped in the cloth. Having to recapture an escaped parrot is not pleasant; escape should be prevented by using vigilance in the first place.

The smaller parrots can be hand-tamed quite quickly. To do this, the wings must first be clipped. Wearing gloves, place the bird gently in position on the gloved hand and hold it in position until it grasps the hand firmly. The bird is then released; it will usually jump off. The bird is recaptured and placed back in position. This is repeated until the bird stops jumping. It is then returned to the cage. The lesson should be repeated at least twice daily. Once the bird becomes accustomed to this handling the gloves can be discarded.

This method is particularly effective with budgies, cockatiels and conures. Frequently they learn to perch on your hand after only one or two lessons.

A parrot that has become thoroughly tame may actually enjoy being handled. Some even like to be roughed up a bit, responding by gently nibbling their owner's hand.

Once tame, a parrot can be taught a wide variety of simple tricks much the way a dog is taught. By watching the bird's natural inclination it will be possible to get ideas for tricks that can be learned. Parrots have been taught to pull miniature wagons, to ring bells, to do somersaults, to walk tightropes, to ride on toys and to do many other amusing things.

Teaching Your Parrot to Talk

Teaching a parrot to talk requires more patience than hand-training, but the reward will be worth the effort. Some kinds of parrots become better talkers than others. If your primary interest in parrots is teaching one to talk, consult the section on the kinds of parrots and choose one of the more easily taught varieties. Young birds become better talkers than mature birds. A really tame parrot will become a better talker than a partially tamed one. Hence, a thorough job of training before you attempt to teach the bird to talk is of great importance.

In teaching a parrot to talk it must be remembered that they are intelligent as birds go, but compared to many other animals they are not very smart. So keep the words or phrases very short and stick to ones with clear, distinct sounds.

Repetition is the key to teaching a parrot to talk. A word or phrase must be repeated constantly over a period of weeks. By the time the bird learns to say the word or phrase you may be so sick of it that you will wish you hadn't started!

Women's and children's voices are more easily imitated than men's voices. Only one voice should do the training, as several different voices will be confusing. If you have a record player you can buy training records that will save you much of the effort of repeating words until the parrot learns them.

Parrots **learn** to talk more readily when there are no distractions. During the training session, the radio and television must be turned off, and if there are other people present, they must remain quiet. Some parrot owners remove even visual distractions by covering the cage during a training session. If, after a training period, the parrot is heard attempting to say the word being taught, the trainer should repeat it promptly to aid the bird in saying it correctly.

It is important to remember that a parrot cannot associate words with meaning. When a parrot says words it is merely imitating the sounds. People are sometimes fooled into believing that a parrot can think when they hear one answering a question. This is just a clever trick. The parrot is first taught the answer and then the question. When both are learned, the bird completes the words it has learned whenever the question is asked.

The first words are the most difficult to teach. Generally speaking, the more words a parrot learns, the more easily it learns, for it is forming the habit of imitating human speech.

Among the parrots that have shown considerable ability to mimic speech are the subspecies of the Yellow-crowned Amazon, *Amazona ochrocephala*. The Double Yellow-head, *A. o. oratrix*, is shown above; on the facing page is the nominate form, *A. o. ochrocephala*.

Breeding

While many kinds of parrots have been bred in captivity, it is difficult to get any of them to breed consistently. If you should be so fortunate as to get a pair to breed, regard it as a happy accident. Nevertheless, if you have a pair of birds, you might as well give it a try.

The first considerations are space and diet. Breeding birds require plenty of room such as is described for aviaries in another section. The diet should be the most wholesome possible. See the section on feeding for details.

Breeding birds insist on privacy. They cannot be expected to produce a family if they are constantly disturbed. Privacy is doubly important once some eggs have been laid. Many a parent has abandoned her clutch because the owner couldn't resist the temptation to peek into the nest box. For most parrots spring is the natural breeding time. In a number of species, both parents care for the eggs and young.

A nest box is essential for breeding. Since most parrots in the wild state breed high up in hollow trees, an effort should be made to simulate a hollow tree. Many boxes are constructed of wood, with the height greater than the width. A hole, just large enough to permit the birds to pass through, should be cut near the top. Because parrots are such good chewers, some people use small garbage pails for nest boxes. Regardless of what is used, there should be a removable top so that the box can be cleaned and so that the inside can, if necessary, be inspected. The bottom of the nest box should be lined with wood shavings, straw or shredded paper.

There are certain signs that indicate the readiness of a pair of birds to breed. One or both may become more active than usual. They will be more attentive to each other. The male may feed the female with food regurgitated from his crop.

In general, the Australian and Asian parrots are more likely to breed in captivity than the African and South American species.

Sexing most species of parrots is difficult since both sexes are formed and colored similarly. Ideally, a number of specimens should be raised together and allowed to pair naturally.

White Cockatoo, *Cacatua alba*, 32 days old.

In the wild many parrots choose to nest in hollows in trees. For the Budgerigar hen raising her brood, the wooden nest box is very similar to natural conditions.

Hand-reared Senegal Parrots, *Poicephalus senegalus*.

Hyacinth Macaw, *Anodorhynchus hyacinthinus*, at 56 days, with two White Cockatoos, *Cacatua alba*, 14 and 15 days old.

Chattering Lories, *Lorius garrulus flavopalliatus*.

Parrot Ailments

Once a parrot has become tame enough to be handled, it should periodically be removed from its cage and carefully examined. Look for injuries, unusual swellings and ingrown feathers. Look carefully under the feathers for mites and lice. Droppings caked on feathers or legs should be washed off. If any unusual signs are noted, the bird should be taken to a veterinarian experienced with birds. (While some vets have had much experience with cage birds, there are others who know little about them.)

Even without an examination, a parrot may appear obviously ill. Some signs of sick birds: the bird sits dejectedly with its feathers fluffed out; diarrhea; irregular or noisy breathing; refusal to eat; swellings or lumps. Since parrots are temperamental birds, they may show some of these symptoms for brief periods without anything serious being wrong, but if they persist, illness must be suspected.

FEATHER-PLUCKING

Parrots that pull out their feathers may have a skin irritation or they may merely be bored. In either case the result can be a bedraggled, unsightly bird. Some birds become habitual feather-pullers; for these usually nothing can be done. The condition should be corrected before it becomes a habit. If it is caused by skin irritation, the cause may be malnutrition. Improved diet and vitamin supplements may help. Irritation can also be caused by mites or lice. This will be discussed more thoroughly later.

If boredom is the cause of feather-plucking, placing small toys and other entertaining objects in the cage may divert the bird. Some aviculturists recommend placing the bird's cage outdoors to give it a new distraction.

FOOT AND BEAK DISORDERS

Disorders of this kind are sometimes not diseases but simple malfunctions. Beaks and claws can grow too long. The keeper must keep them clipped. Some parrots suffer from overgrown beaks, as do some parakeets. If you are hesitant about trimming them, get professional assistance. Use sharp, straight nail nippers. Trimming will not hurt the bird, although there may be a little blood. Before you begin trimming a beak, study a bird with a normal beak or a close-up photo of a bird's head and shape your pet's beak accordingly.

Untrimmed claws can curve back in such a way that the bird cannot grip its perch. Using nail clippers, snip off the tips. Avoid the dark blood vessel running down the inside

Fluffed feathers and a sleepy look are often the first indications of illness the bird keeper notices.

Styptic powder is handy if you clip a claw too short or in case of other minor injuries.

Nervous disorders are often the result of deficient diet. This Budgerigar exhibits a twisting of the neck in addition to the poor claw grip that causes it to hang from its perch.

of the claws; cut short of this. If there is a little bleeding, use a styptic pencil to staunch the flow of blood.

One real foot disease is called bumble foot. This is a painful swelling of the foot caused by wrong diet or lack of exercise. The swelling will have to be relieved by a veterinarian who will lance the swelling to relieve it of pus and a cheeselike secretion.

FRENCH MOLT

Loosely speaking, this is a catch-all term used to designate various feather ailments. Specifically it designates an unnatural condition in which a bird is constantly molting—losing old feathers, growing new ones—so at no one time does the bird appear sleek and fully feathered as it should. Sometimes, too, a false molt will be induced by too much heat or sunlight. Most birds normally molt twice a year—in spring and late summer—for two or three weeks each time. Parrots kept indoors, however, constantly molt a little because of the artificial conditions. But if there is any molting that seems extraordinary, attention should be paid at once, because excessive molting can so weaken a bird that it will soon die.

While the causes of French molt are uncertain, a nutritional deficiency is definitely one of them. This is probably caused by a lack of *animal* protein in the diet. Nearly all birds, in their natural environment, eat some sort of "meat"—insects or worms, for example. Animal protein can be supplied to the cage bird by feeding egg yolk and mealworms; these last are live worms available in pet shops because they are a standard food for some monkeys and tropical fish. Dry dog food has also been used successfully.

The cause of out-of-season molting can also be a mite or bacterial infestation. Try dipping the bird in a very dilute Lysol solution (protecting its head, of course), or give it a liberal spraying with an insecticide specially prepared for birds.

Move the cage of a molting bird to a cooler spot out of strong light. Make sure that it is nowhere near a radiator.

GOING LIGHT

This term is widely used for a bird that is in general decline. It is not a specific ailment. The bird appears to lose substance. When picked up it seems to weigh less. If the cause is not found, the bird is likely to die.

DIARRHEA AND CONSTIPATION

Both of these are symptoms of some other ailment. Sometimes either condition can be remedied by administering a laxative like an eyedropperful of castor oil which will cleanse the intestinal tract. Administering an eyedropperful

Fungal infection on the leg of a lovebird.

Ill birds should be isolated from other birds you may own, as in the case of this White-eyed Conure, *Aratinga leucopthalmus.*

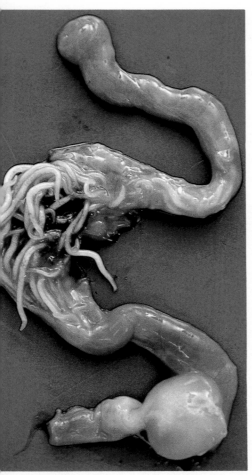

Roundworms in the stomach and small intestine of a parakeet—such parasites are particularly a hazard if parrots are kept outdoors.

Bird louse on the web of a feather; its glassy eggs can be seen beneath it.

of Kaopectate or milk of bismuth three to four hours later, repeated at three hour intervals, will then tend to correct the trouble. Changes in diet can cause diarrhea. If either condition persists, the bird should be taken to a professional experienced with parrots.

PSITTACOSIS, OR PARROT FEVER

This disease warrants more lengthy discussion because it is one of the few bird diseases that can be transmitted to humans. Some people have become so excited over psittacosis that they want all cage birds destroyed. Others, at the other extreme, claim that the disease is a myth. It *is* a real disease; but it is uncommon among cage birds, and it is only rarely contracted by humans.

The disease should more properly be called *ornithosis* because it is found in many other kinds of birds. Pigeons, turkeys, gulls, ducks and chickens are known to be carriers. From 1930 to 1953 only 367 cases of parrot fever were diagnosed in humans in the United States.

While any sick bird should be handled with caution, the parrot owner can feel assured that psittacosis is a rare disease. The 1965 edition of an authoritative medical textbook on virus diseases says: "Psittacosis is a minor health problem." You stand a far greater chance of contracting tuberculosis, typhoid fever, pneumonia or polio from your fellow humans than you do of contracting psittacosis from your pet.

TUMORS

Parrots are as susceptible to tumorous growths as other animals. Old birds are especially likely to acquire them. Tumors on or near the skin can be removed by a veterinarian. Deep tumors are not usually removed, and they are not usually discovered until after the bird is dead.

PARASITES

Individual parrots kept as house pets usually do not have mites and lice because they do not come into contact with other birds, but a newly purchased parrot may have some parasites. When mites or lice are detected, they may be treated with a special insecticide spray purchased from your pet dealer, or the bird may be dusted repeatedly with flowers of sulfur, being careful that it gets down to the skin. Since the cage may harbor mites and lice as well as the birds themselves, the cage should be thoroughly scrubbed with hot soapy water.

BROKEN BONES

If at all possible, wrap a gauze bandage around the body to immobilize the bird and take it to the vet. If you feel competent enough to "do it yourself," follow these instruc-

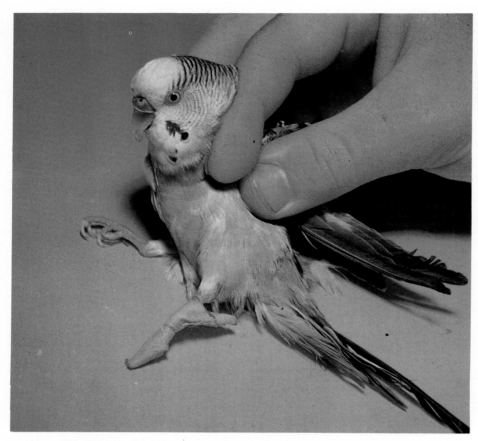

Fractures can be splinted with a variety of materials, depending on the size of the bird.

Self-pluckers often denude their breasts; their heads, of course, remain fully feathered.

Plastic eyedroppers, not glass, should be used to administer medication.

Mite infestation may produce distorted growth of the beak.

tions: If the wing is broken, fold the wing into its natural position with the bone ends touching and wind a one-inch strip of gauze about the body and under the other wing, several times, holding it in place with strips of adhesive tape. Leave it on for about three weeks.

If a leg is broken, make a tiny plaster cast. Use surgeon's plaster, available in drug stores. Have an assistant hold the leg outstretched with the bone ends touching. Apply a thin layer of plaster to the leg, and as it sets, press three half-lengths of flat toothpicks into it, and add a little more plaster. Now wind a narrow strip of gauze around the mass so that it sticks to the adhesive, and hold the bird in position until the cast sets. Allow it to remain in place for three weeks at least. At the end of that time, remove the cast carefully. Vinegar will help to dissolve the plaster.

RESPIRATORY DISEASES

Parrots are subject to colds, pneumonia and clogged nasal passages. As with humans, the best treatment is rest, good diet and avoidance of chills. Antibiotics for birds, available from pet shops, may prove helpful.

A general treatment, suitable in almost all cases, is the application of heat. A bird's temperature is much higher than that of a human, some being normally 109°F. Because of their small size their reserves of fat are limited, and it is a constant struggle for them to maintain their body heat. This is why a sick bird ruffles its feathers. This action creates air pockets which act as insulation. A small bulb kept burning twenty-four hours a day alongside the cage makes a good additional source of heat. (Don't worry about the light preventing the bird from sleeping; it'll just tuck its head back between its wings and will not be bothered in the least.) In extreme cases a towel can be used to cover both cage and bulb to create a heat "tent." Care must be taken to prevent the flammable cloth from touching the bulb. A temperature of 85 to 90°F. maintained this way is extremely beneficial.

In summary, prevention is the best method of combatting disease. Clean surroundings, a nutritious diet and the sense of well-being that comes from tender loving care will go a long way toward preventing most ailments.

Popular Parrots

Unlike the Scarlet Macaw, the Green-winged (above) and the Blue-and-Gold (facing page) have prominent lines of small feathers in the facial patch.

MACAWS

These natives of Central and South America are the largest members of the parrot tribe. Travelers along the waterways of the South American rain forests are accustomed to seeing these brilliantly colored birds flying high overhead, their loud cries being heard until they are out of sight.

Macaws adapt easily to captivity, but because of their size, they should be considered only by those with an aviary or some other spacious way of keeping them. If they are kept in an aviary, the frame must be of sturdy metal and the wire must be heavy—on the order of chain link fence—because the macaws have tremendous chewing strength in their beaks. Macaws are sometimes kept tethered to a parrot stand, but this seems a little cruel to most people. A tamed macaw can be kept on a parrot stand if its wings have been clipped.

If they are mistreated, macaws can be loud, vicious birds. Treated with kindness, they may develop genuine affection for their owners. They sometimes become nearly as devoted as dogs.

Macaws are not good talkers. Those who keep them do so usually because of their bright colors, their ability to learn tricks and their sense of devotion. Long-lived, one macaw in captivity is known to have reached the age of sixty-four.

Blue-and-Gold Macaw, *Ara ararauna*. Panama to the Guianas and Paraguay. These almost yard-long birds are deep sky blue on the head, back, wings and tail. Neck, breast and undersurface of wings are rich golden. Throat and beak are black. Nearly white facial patches are marked with lines of black feathers.

Green-winged Macaw, *Ara chloroptera*. Panamanian peninsula south to the tropical rain forests of South America. As large as the Blue-and-Gold Macaw, the Green-winged is predominantly colored a brilliant red. The wings are made up of blue and green feathers. Rump is blue. Tail feathers are red with blue tips. The nearly white facial patches are marked with lines of small red feathers.

Scarlet Macaw, *Ara macao*. Mexico south to tropical rain forests of central South America. The Scarlet is a bit smaller than the Green-winged, but much of the plumage is also red. The wings are colored with yellow, green and blue. The tail is scarlet, tipped with pale blue. The small

red feathers on the cream-colored facial patch are hardly noticeable.

Hyacinth Macaw, *Anodorhynchus hyacinthinus*. Brazil. Measuring forty inches from head to tip of tail, the Hyacinth Macaw is the largest of all parrots. It is cobalt-blue overall, with the underside of the tail dark gray. There is a bare, yellow patch surrounding the lower mandible.

AFRICAN GREY PARROT

African Grey Parrot, *Psittacus erithacus*. West central Africa. About thirteen inches long. The only member of the genus *Psittacus*. A red tail contrasts sharply with the overall gray plumage. This is probably the best talker of all the parrots. Only the Panama and Double Yellow-headed Amazons come close to it. Because of strict import regulations, the African Grey is not common in the United States, and it is expensive. Many of the African Greys put up for sale are mature birds, but this is not a serious deterrent, since one may live for fifty years or more. Young Greys have gray irises which become pale yellow as the bird matures. They breed fairly readily in captivity, and they usually make excellent pets.

CONURES

The most commonly seen conures are those of the genus *Aratinga*. They are closely related to the macaws, which they strongly resemble except for size. Conures are smaller than most macaws. A quick way to distinguish them is to note the amount of bare skin on the face. In most macaws the whole cheek appears to be without feathers, whereas in the conures only a narrow area around the eye lacks feathers. Many species occur throughout Central and South America and the Caribbean Islands. They are frequently available in pet stores in the United States. Conures are only fair talkers, but they make affectionate pets. They have a fairly long, pointed tail.

Orange-fronted Conure, *Aratinga canicularis*. This nine-and-a-half-inch parrot from western Central America is green overall, with a band of orange on the forehead and yellowish eye rings. The bill is horn-colored. Orange-fronted Conures make fine pets if they are bought when young or if they have already been tamed.

Aztec Conure, *Aratinga nana astec*. Eastern Central America. A little larger than the Orange-fronted, the Aztec is also a green bird. Its beak and eye ring are smaller than the Orange-fronted's, and it lacks the pronounced orange forehead. It too has a horn-colored bill.

Brown-throated Conure, *Aratinga pertinax*. Several subspecies occur in Panama and northern South America. Less colorful than some of the other conures, the Brown-

In the course of a bird show, a Hyacinth Macaw plays dead.

The bright red tail distinguishes the nominate subspecies of the African Grey from the maroon-tailed *P. e. timneh*.

Orange-fronted Conure—the orange restricted from the eye by blue continuing onto the lores characterizes the subspecies *clarae*.

Jandaya Conure (above); Double Yellow-headed Amazon (below); Brown-throated Conure (facing page)—this specimen appears to be the subspecies *aeruginosa*.

throated is mostly green. Face, cheeks, throat and bill are brownish. Brown-throats make good pets.

Jandaya Conure, *Arantinga jandaya*. Northeastern Brazil. Twelve inches long. More colorful than most conures, the Jandaya has a yellow head and neck, an orange-red breast and abdomen and some blue mixed in with the green on the rest of its body. The yellow areas are tinged with orange, and the bill is gray-black. The Jandaya is very popular as a pet.

Sun Conure, *Aratinga solstitialis*. The Guianas, southeast Venezuela and northeast Brazil. Approximately the same size as the Jandaya Conure, and even more colorful. The overall plumage is yellow, with areas on the head, abdomen and lower back tinged with orange. The wings are yellow, green and blue. The bill is gray.

Nanday Conure, *Nandayus nenday*. Southeast Bolivia, southern Brazil and Paraguay and northern Argentina. This twelve-inch bird is the only member of its genus. One of the most attractive conures, the Nanday has a black head and bill, blue-black wing feathers and red thighs. The underside of the tail is black, while the upper side is bluish green; the rest of the bird is yellowish green, with some blue on the chest. Properly trained, the Nanday makes a good pet.

THE GENUS BROTOGERIS

The genus *Brotogeris* has many species throughout Central and South America, one of which is commonly sold and one other is occasionally available.

Orange-chinned Parakeet, *B. jugularis*. Mexico to northern Colombia and Venezuela. Only six-and-a-half inches long, the little Orange-chinned, or Beebee, Parakeet is a popular pet. Dark green on top, lighter underneath, with a bright orange spot on the chin. Sometimes a good talker.

Golden-winged Parakeet, *B. chrysopterus*. Venezuela, the Guianas and parts of Brazil. Similar to the Orange-chinned, but less often seen in pet shops. Green overall, with some orange and blue on the wings. Has a white eye ring.

AMAZON PARROTS

All amazon parrots belong to the genus *Amazona*, which comprises a very large group of medium-sized, colorful birds. Many of them become excellent talkers.

Yellow-crowned Amazon, *A. ochrocephala*. From Central Mexico south to the Amazon River area in Brazil; eastern Peru and Trinidad. Fourteen inches. The nine subspecies are basically green and yellow birds, the amount of yellow varying with each subspecies. Four members of the genus are particularly noted for their ability to mimic human speech and learn tricks.

Panama Amazon, *A. o. panamensis*. Panama to Colombia. This is a typically green parrot, with yellow on the head and red on the shoulder and primaries. Although Panamas are not spectacular in coloring, they make up for it admirably by being gifted talkers and imitators of other sounds.

Yellow-naped Amazon, *A. o. auropalliata*. Mexico to northeast Costa Rica. A green bird with a band of yellow on the back of the neck and a patch of yellow about the beak. Some red and blue on the wings. The Yellow-naped is an ideal pet; it's easily trained and a good talker.

Double Yellow-headed Amazon, *A. o. oratrix*. Mexico to Central America. Mature specimens of this popular parrot have yellow heads and necks. In immature specimens the yellow is confined to a small area on the forehead. The yellow spreads with age to the balance of the head and neck. Body and wings are green, with some blue on the wings. At the base of the tail is a patch of bright red. A very good talker.

Single Yellow-headed Amazon, *A. o. ochrocephala*. Central America and northern half of South America. Color bright green, bright yellow on the head, red across the wings and at the base of the tail. Frequently a very good talker.

Green-cheeked Amazon, *A. viridigenalis*. Mexico. About thirteen inches long. A green parrot, especially bright on the cheeks. Top of the head is red, and there is a red band in the wings. The red area increases with age. Fair talkers, but inclined to be noisy.

Blue-fronted Amazon, *A. aestiva*. Brazil, Paraguay, Argentina. Fifteen inches. Predominantly green, with light blue on the forehead; crown, cheeks and throat yellow. Some red on the wings. Very popular in Europe, less so in the United States.

White-fronted Amazon, *A. albifrons*. Mexico and Central America. With a length of ten inches, this is one of the smaller Amazons. A bright green bird, with white on the front of the head and blue on the back of the head. Red feathers surround the eye and extend to the base of the beak. A fair talker. Apt to be noisy.

Cuban Amazon, *A. leucocephala*. Cuba, Bahamas and nearby islands. Length to thirteen inches. A very pretty parrot. Rich green overall, with white forehead and pink on the throat and cheeks. The abdomen and base of the tail are tinged with wine color. The green wings are marked with bright blue. Very active birds, and quite noisy. Not very good talkers.

LOVEBIRDS

Lovebirds, which come from Africa, are desirable because they are hardy, long-lived, breed well in captivity

Amazon parrots: Orange-winged, *A. amazonica* (above); White-fronted, *A. albifrons* (below).

This young Yellow-naped Amazon so far shows yellow
only on the forehead; that on the nape has yet to appear.

Of all the lovebird species, the Peach-faced is probably
the best known and most widely bred.

In captivity many lovebird species have been allowed to interbreed —the birds shown above are hybrids of the Peach-faced and the Masked (below).

and are adept at learning tricks. Lovebirds get their common name from the affection and devotion pairs of them show each other.

These diminutive birds (they're only about six inches long) are readily bred in captivity. Because of their aggressiveness, they should not be kept with other kinds of birds.

If breeding is desired, lovebirds should be given a nest box twelve inches high by six inches square. A two-inch hole should be cut near the top, which should be removable for cleaning. Lovebirds are very ambitious nest builders, so most species should be provided with quantities of grass, straw, twigs, leaves and bark. Once egg-laying begins, an egg is usually laid every other day until up to eight are laid. Incubation lasts about three weeks. Since the eggs may be laid over a period of more than two weeks, the young will hatch over a similar period.

In some species it is difficult to distinguish the sexes. Matters are not improved by the fact that two females will sometimes build a nest and lay eggs, and two males may also build a nest.

Of the nine species of lovebirds, only three species are commonly sold in the United States.

Peach-faced Lovebird, *Agapornis roseicollis*. Southwest Africa. Breeds readily. Body color is bright green; face and breast peach; rump bright blue. The horn-colored bill is tinged with green.

Masked Lovebird, *Agapornis personata*. Tanzania. Good breeders. The body is green, paler on the abdomen. Entire head is black; breast and back of neck are yellow. The white eye ring is especially prominent because of the black head. The bill is red.

Blue Masked Lovebird. A color variant of the Masked Lovebird and thus the same species. Head is black and the rest of the bird is blue. There is no yellow, as in the Normal Masked.

Fischer's Lovebird, *Agapornis fischeri*. Vicinity of Lake Victoria in northern Tanzania. Bright green body; head orange, becoming paler on the neck, throat and breast. Rump blue; beak red. White eye ring prominent.

COCKATOOS

Cockatoos are extremely handsome birds native to Australia and the surrounding islands. On the top of its head, each cockatoo has a crest which can be raised or lowered at will. The size of the crest varies from species to species. In the farming regions of Australia, cockatoos are very unpopular because large flocks of them descend upon farm fields to feed on grain. It is unfortunate that Australia's strict exportation laws make them scarce in the

United States, because they make excellent pets and some of them are good talkers. Fortunately, several species of cockatoos are being bred in captivity in the United States.

Greater Sulphur-crested Cockatoo, *Cacatua galerita*. Australia and neighboring islands. There are records of Greater Sulphur-crested Cockatoos living well over 100 years. These large (twenty inches) snow-white birds have bright yellow crests. Probably the most popular of all the cockatoos.

Lesser Sulphur-crested Cockatoo, *Cacatua sulphurea*. Celebes and adjacent islands. Similar to the Greater Sulphur-crested, but smaller (thirteen inches).

Major Mitchell's Cockatoo, *Cacatua leadbeateri*. Australian interior. This large bird (fourteen inches) is beautiful. Head, neck, breast and belly are pink. Wings, back and tail are white. The very large crest is pink, rose-red and yellow. Also known as Leadbeater's Cockatoo. An excellent talker.

Long-billed Corella, *Cacatua tenuirostris*. Inland southwestern and southeastern Australia. The body is white, with some orange-red on the head, throat and breast. A rather long upper mandible becomes longer with age and will occasionally have to be trimmed. An affectionate pet and a good talker.

Moluccan Cockatoo, *Cacatua moluccensis*. Molucca Islands of Indonesia. Overall plumage is pale salmon-pink. The crest is a darker salmon-pink color. Also called Salmon-crested Cockatoo. A fine pet and a good talker.

Rose-breasted Cockatoo, *Eolophus roseicapillus*. Australian interior. Forehead and crest pale pink; deeper pink under the wings and on the face, neck and breast. The rest of the bird is colored varying shades of gray. Also known as the Galah. Can be an affectionate pet and a good talker.

COCKATIEL

Cockatiel, *Nymphicus hollandicus*. A smaller relative of the cockatoos, the cockatiel averages about twelve inches in length and is native to Australia. The prominent color is gray, with a yellow face and crest. In the center of the yellow patch is a large orange spot. The wings have a large white patch. Females generally lack the orange spot and have barred outer tail feathers. Immature males resemble females.

Cockatiels make fine pets. They are plentiful and relatively inexpensive in the United States. They become fair talkers, although their high-pitched voices make them a little hard to understand. They also can learn to whistle tunes.

Cockatoos: Major Mitchell's and Greater Sulphur-crested (above); Lesser Sulphur-crested (below)— the larger is the subspecies *citrinocristata*.

Salmon-crested, or Moluccan, Cockatoo.

Eclectus Parrot pair—the furlike quality of the plumage
has drawn the attention of many fanciers.

Parrots of the Pacific distribution: Western Rosella (above); Red-rumped Parakeet cock (below).

BUDGERIGAR

Budgerigar, *Melopsittacus undulatus*. Australia. The wild Budgerigar is a green and yellow bird with a yellow face and forehead, black and yellow barring on the back, black spots across the throat and a green breast. These birds breed readily in captivity and there are now many different color varieties available.

Probably the best known and most popular of all parrots, this small (about seven inches) bird is an ideal pet. Budgerigars are friendly, easy to care for and inexpensive. They also can learn to talk and do tricks, although some people believe that males (which have blue ceres) are better for training than females (which have brownish ceres).

ROSELLAS

Rosellas are very colorful birds, popular more as aviary birds than as pets. They are well-proportioned birds with long, broad tails and a black shoulder patch and scalloped feathers on the back.

Crimson Rosella, *Platycercus elegans*. Eastern and southeastern Australia. Thirteen inches long. A crimson bird with cheek patches, central tail feathers and edges of wing feathers violet-blue. The back is black, and wing feathers are edged with crimson.

Western Rosella, *Platycercus icterotis*. Southwestern Australia. Ten inches long. Head and breast red, yellow cheek patches. Black back, and wing feathers edged with green. Some blue on the wings, and green and blue tail feathers.

ECLECTUS PARROTS

Eclectus Parrot, *Eclectus roratus*. South Pacific Islands and New Guinea. These large (fourteen inches) birds are brilliantly colored and sexually dimorphic. Males are basically green birds with red patches on the sides of the breast and red under the wings. Females are basically red birds with blue around the nape and on the abdomen. An Eclectus Parrot can make a fine pet and can learn to talk. Females are usually shyer than males.

THE GENUS PSEPHOTUS

Members of the genus *Psephotus* are attractive birds averaging about eleven inches in length. All come from Australia.

Blue-bonnet, *P. haematogaster*. Brown-gray bird with blue on the forehead extending to the chin. Abdomen yellow and red; upper side of tail black.

Red-rumped Parakeet, *P. haematonotus*. Red rump; yellow abdomen; yellow, blue and green on the wings. The green on the rest of the bird is tinged with brown and, in some places, blue. Has a particularly pleasant whistle.

THE GENUS POLYTELIS

Members of this genus are medium-sized birds (about seventeen inches long) with long tapering tails. Native to Australia, they are expensive in the United States.

Superb Parakeet, *P. swainsonii*. A generally green bird with yellow on the forehead, cheeks and throat. There is a band of red below the yellow on the throat. Also known as the Barraband Parakeet.

Princess Parakeet, *P. alexandrae*. A bird of subtle colors. Light blue crown; pink on the chin, throat and thighs. The blue-gray on the breast and abdomen is tinged with yellow and green. Varying shades of yellow-green on the rest of the bird, with some blue on the wings.

THE GENUS NEOPHEMA

All of the species in this genus are native to Australia. Because of their habits of feeding, all of the neophemas are referred to as grass parakeets.

Elegant Parakeet, *N. elegans*. The basic olive coloring of this approximately nine-inch bird is tinged with yellow on the face, breast and abdomen. The frontal band is dark blue with a longer band of light blue bordering it on the forehead. The wings are olive, blue and black. Breeds well in captivity.

Bourke's Parakeet, *N. bourkii*. A bit smaller than the Elegant, Bourke's Parakeet is basically a pale rose-colored bird with a blue frontal band and blue on the wings and rump and under the tail. These parakeets have been widely bred in captivity, and there are now a few color varieties.

THE GENUS PSITTACULA

Some of the most popular aviary birds are in the genus *Psittacula*. These long, pointed-tailed birds are generally pastel-colored. Most males are distinguished by their red bills. These parakeets are generally more popular because of their beautiful colors rather than for their trainability, though they can be tamed and can make fine pets.

Plum-headed Parakeet, *P. cyanocephala*. Ceylon and India. About thirteen inches long. Generally a green-colored bird, the Plum-head has a blue tail tipped with white. The chin is black, as is the band of color around the neck. There is also a blue-green band on the neck. As the common name implies, the head color is plum.

Rose-ringed Parakeet, *P. krameri*. Central and northeastern Africa, Afghanistan and Nepal south to Ceylon and east to Burma. Sixteen inches long. The pastel green of this bird is accented by a black line from cere to eyes, a black chin and partial band of black from the chin across the lower cheeks and a band of rose on the back of the neck. The green on the back of the neck is tinged with blue.

Superb Parakeet cock (above); Bourke's Parakeet hen (below); Plum-headed Parakeet pair (facing page).

Black-headed Caique—caiques are renowned for their
playful and charming behavior.

White-bellied Caique (above);
Rainbow Lory, subspecies *moluc-
canus* (below).

Moustached Parakeet, *P. alexandri*. India and **Nepal** east to southern China; also Sumatra and nearby islands. Thirteen inches long. Breast and upper abdomen deep salmon; chin and lower cheeks black; head blue-gray. **A** black band stretches across the forehead eye to eye. The rest of the bird is green, tinged in some places with blue **or** yellow.

CAIQUES

Caiques are interesting, intelligent and amusing birds from northern South America. They have short, square tails.

Black-headed Caique, *Pionites melanocephala*. Nine inches long. Crown and back of neck black; cheeks and throat orange-yellow. There is a bit of green under the eye. Breast and abdomen white. Sides of abdomen and thighs orange. Wings are green and violet-blue. Black bill.

White-bellied Caique, *Pionites leucogaster*. Same size as the Black-headed. Crown and back of neck orange; throat and sides of the head yellow; breast and abdomen white. The thighs are green, and the wings are green and violet-blue. Bill is horn-colored.

LORIES AND LORIKEETS

Lories and lorikeets are unusual birds in that they have specially structured tongues for feeding primarily on pollen and nectar. Most of these birds are brilliantly colored, and all are native to the South Pacific.

Rainbow Lory, *Trichoglossus haematodus*. About ten and a half inches long. The black head has purple highlights on the forehead, forecrown and chin. On the back of the neck is a band of yellow, and the red breast is barred with black. Abdomen dark green, thighs yellow barred with dark green, and back green. Underside of wings red-orange, yellow and dark green. The twenty-one subspecies vary somewhat in color. Can make affectionate and amusing pets.

Chattering Lory, *Lorius garrulus*. Twelve inches long. Overall plumage red. Wings and thighs green. Bend of wing yellow. Tail is black. Chattering Lories, one of the most frequently available, make comical pets.

A Technician's View of Handling Birds and Performing Routine Physical Exams

Missy Meers, Miki Roche,
Maggie Parhm, and Susan Gibson
Animal Health Technicians
at Atlanta Animal Hospital, Dunwoody, Georgia

Pet birds are not difficult to handle. However, they are easily injured and can cause a great deal of pain and injury to the inexperienced handler. Before taking a bird out of its cage, cut off escape routes by closing doors and windows. Birds adapt slowly to changes in light, so turning out room lights should make the bird easy to catch. Small birds such as parakeets can be caught bare-handed and held in the palm of your hand, holding the head either between thumb and forefinger or between forefinger and middle finger. By cupping your hand you can both support its back and also hold its wings.

Larger birds may be caught with gloves or a towel. Many birds become glove-shy while in quarantine—a towel may work better. Wrap the bird in the towel, holding the back of its head through the towel. Let it chew contentedly at the fabric to take its mind off what you are doing. Wings or feet are easy to unwrap for feather-trims or nail-trims. Although some birds use their beaks aggressively (stocks, particularly, aim to put your eyes out), birds of prey such as hawks defend themselves with their feet and can easily pierce your wrist with their talons—control their feet first.

Birds have no diaphragm. If you apply pressure to the breast (keel bone) and inhibit thoracic movement, a bird may rapidly asphyxiate. Birds also have an unusual breathing system composed of lungs and air sacs—they do not cough or sneeze well. After giving a bird medicine, give it its head so it can shake out any excess liquid, or it may choke or inhale the medicine.

If a bird escapes your hold, first check that all exits are closed, then turn off the lights. The bird will generally fly to the floor or a convenient perch. Be careful of back-lit glass such as a window into the next room, as the bird may fly toward the light and hit the window glass. A bird on a hard-to-reach perch may step onto a stick placed before its legs. We recommend against using nets, as it is easy for a bird tangled in a net to break a wing or leg.

A Cockatiel restrained by holding its head between thumb and forefinger. Palpation of the abdomen can give an indication of a hen's breeding condition.

Chart #1 Avian History Form

I. History

  A. Identification

    _____ Name_____ Age _____ Sex _____ Species _____

       Color _____ Weight

  B. Symptoms

     1. Major complaint _____

     2. Duration _____

     3. Appetite _____ Normal _____Reduced _____ Anorexia

     4. Dropping

       a. Appearance _____ Dark with white center _____ Light with white scattered

          _____ Other

       b. Number _____ < 25 _____ 25 to 50 _____ > 50

       c. Consistency _____ firm _____ soft

     5. Regurgitation _____ yes _____ no

     6. Water consumption _____ Decreased _____ Normal _____ Increased

     7. Activity _____Decreased _____ Normal _____Increased

     8. Respiration _____ sneezing or coughing _____ tail fluking

         _____ open mouth breathing

         _____ wheezing _____increased rate

     9. Prior illness and medication _____

  C. Environment

     1. Cage and location

       _____ new cage   _____ excessive sunlight

       _____ new cage location   _____ presence of mirror

       _____ drafts (air-conditioning & heating)   _____ cage sanitation

       _____ paint chipped from cage   _____ destruction of toys
                                                                       — too many toys

     2. Aerosal use

       _____ insecticides _____ paint fumes _____ other

     3. Duration of ownership _____

       Where purchased   _____

     4. Other family pets   _____

     5. Feed and Minerals

       Type   _____

       Amount feed   _____

       Location of feeder   _____

       Feed additives _____ Codliver oil _____ Vitamins _____ Treats

                    _____ Calcium _____ Greens _____ Other

                    _____ Iodine _____ Fruits

       Feed freshness _____

     6. Water

       How often replaced _____ Location _____

       Water sanitation   _____.

       Watering vehicle   _____ Other _____

After obtaining a complete history of the bird's nutrition, management, and problems (see chart #1), observe the bird in its cage. Look for fluffed feathers, tail fluking (tail lifting to assist breathing, a sign of dyspnea), nasal or ocular discharge, unusual number or character of droppings, lameness or other postural abnormalities, lethargy, and so forth. Catch the bird and take its temperature before it gets excited and its body temperature rises. Lift the tail to expose the vent and insert the thermometer no more than about 1 cm. Pediatric rectal thermometers work well. A normal bird's temperature is more than 39 °C. (103 °F.) Add 1 ° if the bird is excited. There are a few species with a different temperature range, but you are unlikely to encounter them in practice—a healthy penguin may have a temperature of 43 °C. (110 °F.). An excited macaw may blush, so don't worry if its cheeks turn red.

If feathers are dull and lifeless, the bird may have a nutritional deficiency. Check the "wing-pits" for small red or dark feather mites. In a feather plucker, note the location of plucked feathers. If feathers have been plucked from the back of the head and neck, another bird is probably doing the plucking. Check the eyes, using an ophthalmoscope if necessary. Touch the beak to get the bird to open its mouth and check for ulcers or scabs. Check the legs and cere for crusty, honey-combed skin which may be due to scaly-leg mites (verify with a microscope). Feel the crop and see if it is empty or full to gauge whether the bird has just eaten and to check for foreign bodies in the crop. Feel the keel bone—the muscle should be level with the edge of the keel. Atrophy indicates weight loss. Check for lumps and bumps. The uropygial, or preen, gland on top of the tail base can become impacted like a dog's anal glands and may need to be expressed. In listening to the heart and lungs use a stethoscope with a rubber ring to avoid background sound of feathers rubbing on the stethoscope. When a bird is standing, its heart is located approximately between its legs. Listen to both left and right sides of the chest and be alert for arrhythmias. The lungs are attached to the dorsal ribs—listen along the back. Listen further caudally to the air sacs. Admittedly the veterinarian is going to be doing the physical exam on most clients' birds. However, you will be helping, and you will probably be examining birds that are hospitalized daily. Your ability to perform a competent physical exam on a bird will be of considerable value to your hospital.

Weigh each bird accurately (see chart #2). Weight is an important part of the base-line data. A scale with a weighing basket (Ohaus Scale Corp., Florham Park, New Jersey) works best. Tape up the holes to keep the bird calm

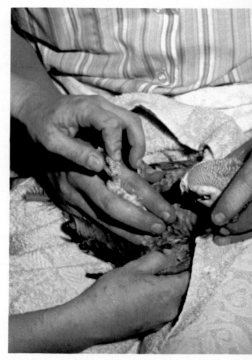

Restraint of larger parrots, such as this African Grey, may require two people (above). A Budgerigar, however, often needs to be held only loosely (facing page, below). Gloves are used to hold a Nanday Conure for claw clipping (facing page, above).

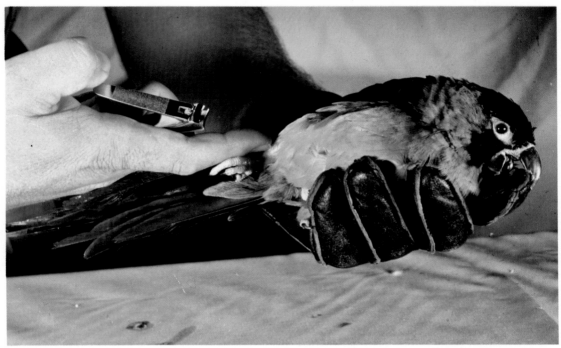

and to prevent it from hooking its beak or claws in the holes. An inaccurate weight is not worth taking with an animal that weighs as little as most birds. Hospitalized birds, particularly if they are not eating and are being tube-fed, should probably be weighed daily to assess their recovery. Try to weigh at the same time each day, before feeding.

None of the procedures discussed above should take any longer in a bird than they would in a dog or cat, and they are just as critical to proper care in birds as in any other animals.

Chart #2 Average Avian Weights

Hummingbirds	2.4–5 gm.
Mannikins	5–11 gm.
Java Sparrow	24–30 gm.
Canary	18–38 gm.
House Sparrow	27 gm.
Budgerigar	35–60 gm.
Masked Lovebird	62 gm.
Fischer's Lovebird	55–70 gm.
Glossy Starling	80 gm.
Blue-crowned Conure	92 gm.
Ring-neck Parakeet	155 gm.
Greater Indian Hill Mynah	180–260 gm.
Domestic Pigeon	240–300 gm.
Crow	340 gm.
African Grey Parrot	360 gm.

This chart is very sketchy, as little work has been done on average weights in normal birds.

Diagnostic Laparoscopy in Birds

William C. Satterfield, D.V.M.

What is laparoscopy?

Laparoscopy is a procedure for examining the spaces within the body without major surgical invasion of those spaces. The laparoscope is an instrument developed over twenty years ago for use in human medicine. Since the late 1960's, the miniaturized laparoscope—which employs a fiberoptic system—and accompanying instruments have been used by physicians in procedures such as examination of the unborn fetus and the knee in humans. Application of the laparoscope to bird sexing came in the earliest phase of its veterinary use.

Light from a remote source of illumination travels through a small, flexible glass-filled tubing to a viewing tip with an eyepiece. The light level is adjustable to allow the veterinarian to select the best illumination for the procedure. Most laparoscopes contain a magnification system which enlarges the final image up to thirty times, allowing close-up, detailed examination of the surface of the organs. Viewing tips are available in various sizes, but avian laparoscopy is often done with a 2.2 mm diameter (14 gauge) tip, which is about the size of a large hypodermic needle.

Why are birds laparoscoped?

Birds are laparoscoped to determine their sex and breeding condition, to examine the internal organs for signs of disease, and to take small tissue samples for microscopic study. In sexually monomorphic species (those in which the male and female show no external differences) laparoscopy is the most common procedure for sex determination. With the world population of all wild animals decreasing rapidly and with federal regulations restricting the importation of many species, captive breeding programs have become increasingly important. Pairing birds of confirmed sex and in good breeding condition can be the most important key to a successful avian propagation program.

Procedure for sex determination by laparoscopy

For most species, an assistant restrains the bird manually on its right side by holding the wings together over the back and gently extending the legs. If anesthesia is used, a second assistant monitors the bird's breathing and heart rate.

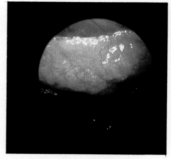

Immature ovary of a young amazon parrot.

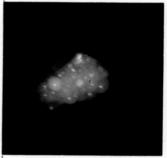

Inactive ovary of an amazon parrot—note undeveloped follicles.

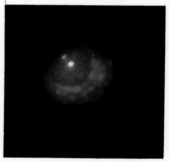

Ovary of parrot, showing a developing follicle.

Ovary of parrot, with a more mature follicle.

Dual light source for the laparoscope. The light controls on the left are for photography, the controls on the right for general examining use.

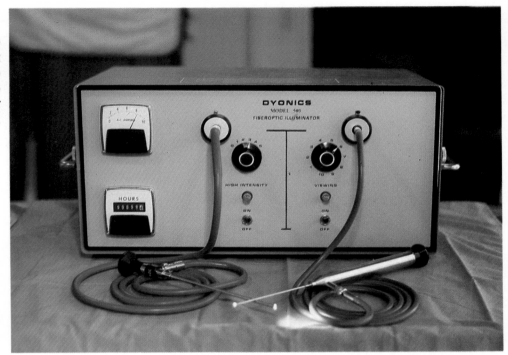

Portable light source with laparoscope, cannula and trochars.

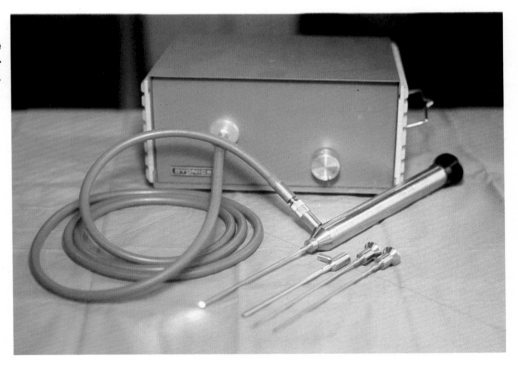

Two laparoscopes compared for diameter with a 16-gauge hypodermic needle.

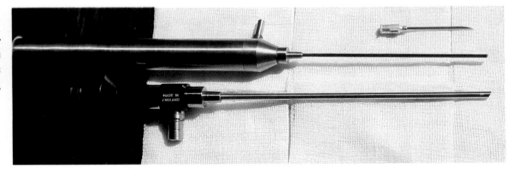

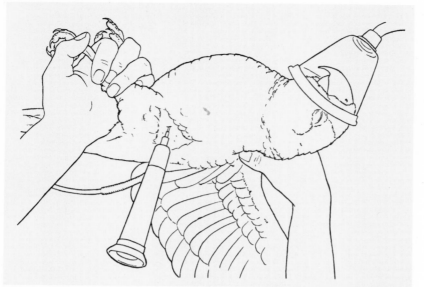

A small skin area on the bird's left side is prepared for sterile surgery. The landmarks for locating the optimum area for the procedure are the last rib, the ilium, and the proximal half of the femur. Within the triangle formed by these, a small incision is carefully made through the skin and superficial muscle. This is no more traumatic than giving a hypodermic injection and generally produces no noticeable discomfort to the bird. The hollow sleeve, or *cannula*, containing a sharp pointed rod, the *trochar*, is inserted into the abdominal air sac. The trochar is then removed from the cannula, and the viewing tip of the laparoscope with its light-carrying bundles and optical system is inserted. For birds weighing less than 100 grams, the laparoscope may be inserted directly through the incision without using the cannula, which reduces the diameter of the instrument to 1.7 mm.

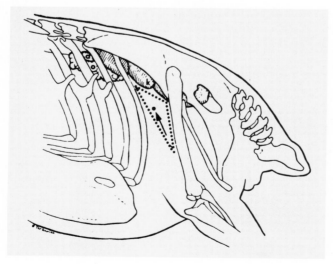

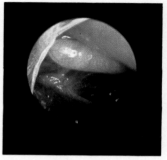

The white organ in the center is the testicle of a Crowned Crane.

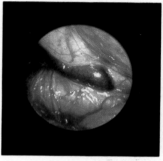

The dark organ has the normal color of a testicle of a Glossy Ibis.

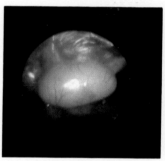

The white organ in the center is a mature, active testicle of an African Grey Parrot.

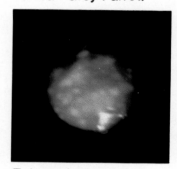

Tuberculosis lesions in the liver of a turaco.

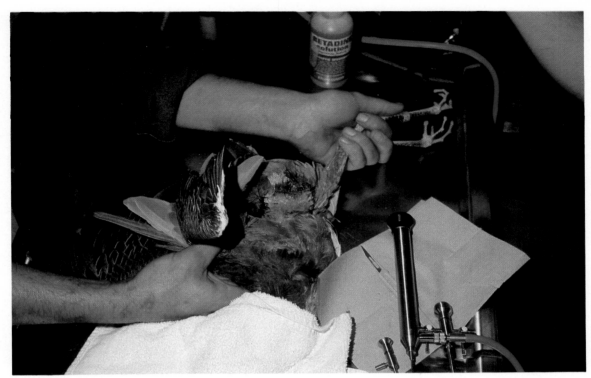

A night heron being
prepared for sexing.

When properly placed, the viewing tip of the laparoscope will be near the anterior (uppermost) lobe of the left kidney, and the gonad will be seen just above this point, attached to the adrenal gland. Identification of the gonad is completed in about one minute, and the laparoscope and cannula are withdrawn. A topical antibiotic powder is placed on the small puncture; sutures are not required.

Whether the examination is done in a veterinary hospital or at an aviary, the laparoscopic equipment is thoroughly cleaned and sterilized before each bird is examined so there is no danger of infection. Liquid or gas sterilization is used since steam-and-heat sterilization is damaging to the lens system of the laparoscope.

What does the veterinarian see when a bird is laparoscoped?

The ovary in a female bird is a cluster of hundreds of round follicles, each containing an undeveloped ovum. A young bird will have relatively small, uniform follicles. A female bird in breeding condition will show a large developing follicle or a mature follicle just prior to ovulation and egg formation.

The male bird has a smooth, dense testicle, either pale or dark. The veterinarian can evaluate the bird's breeding condition by the size of the testicle and its blood supply. Development and activity of the gonads can be correlated with behavioral data to indicate the bird's response to environmental, nutritional, and husbandry conditions.

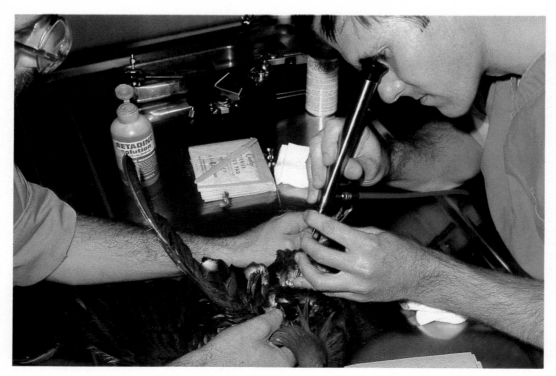

A Nicobar Pigeon is laparoscoped for sex

Are there other ways of determining the bird's sex?

In waterfowl and poultry, *vent sexing* remains one of the most useful and rapid techniques for sexing newly hatched young. Many aviculturists effectively utilize this easy-to-learn method. However, there are many other avian species for which this technique is not effective. In these species, aviculturists have paired birds "naturally" by behavioral characteristics. Unfortunately, there is room for error in this method, and many individuals have been paired with another of the same sex.

A modification of the caponizing procedure (*laparotomy*) has been used in various ways to allow direct visualization of the gonads via a small incision and the use of an otoscope or small speculum. This is an effective technique, but it has not gained wide acceptance because size of the surgical incision is relatively large and its application is limited to sexing.

Two nonsurgical techniques for sexing monomorphic birds include *sex chromosome determination* and *fecal steroid analysis*. Both procedures involve a uniquely equipped laboratory and are quite expensive and time consuming. Until recently, fecal steroid laboratory services have been limited primarily to endangered species in large collections, but are now commercially available through local veterinarians in the U.S.

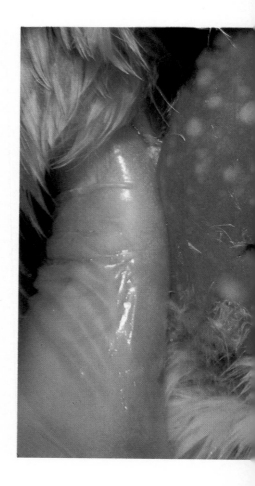

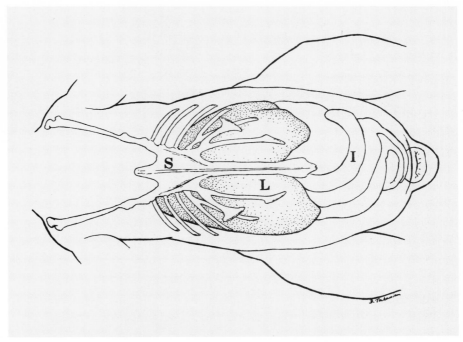

Lateral topography of the ventral skeleton and viscera with the needlescope inserted for examination of the liver. *L*, liver; *S*, sternum; *I*, intestine.

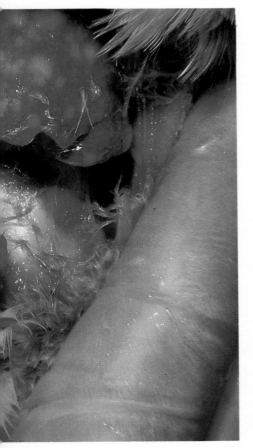

Avian tuberculosis in the liver of a Wood Duck.

Are there other uses for avian laparoscopy?

In addition to its use in sex determination, laparoscopy is a versatile diagnostic tool. The air sacs and posterior surface of the lungs may be examined for signs of infection. The kidneys, adrenals, spleen, intestines, and liver may be rapidly evaluated visually, and samples taken for bacteriologic culture or histopathologic study under the microscope. Information about the bird's health is available in a short time without major surgery.

An increasingly common procedure is the liver biopsy. Biopsy results can be of major assistance to the manager of a large or valuable collection that has had a problem with avian tuberculosis, viral hepatitis, amyloidosis, or an inclusion-body disease. This technique can provide rapid and accurate answers about the status of an individual bird without endangering its health, and the manager can use this information to select birds for quarantine or entry into the collection.

When the liver is to be examined, the bird is placed on its back with its feet held back. The laparoscope with a biopsy attachment is inserted through the abdominal tissue directly behind the sternum in the midline. The surgeon can view most surfaces of the liver and can even examine the heart in some cases. If abnormal tissue is seen on the surface of the liver, the surgeon can take a small portion of this tissue to be sent to the laboratory for microscopic examination. The laparoscope is withdrawn, and a topical antibiotic is placed on the small skin wound. A single suture may sometimes be placed in the skin.

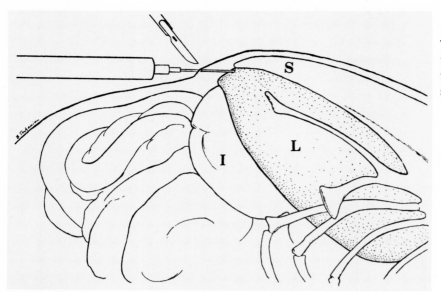

Topography of the ventral skeleton and superficial viscera. *L*, liver; *S*, sternum; *I*, intestine.

Conclusion

Laparoscopy, one of the major recent advances in the science of avian medicine, is an important conservation and husbandry technique and diagnostic tool. It is a rapid, safe, noninjurious procedure that allows direct visual observation of the gonads and examination and sampling of the abdominal organs in a living bird. Used as an adjunct to other techniques, laparoscopy has significant applications in the management and conservation of avian species in captivity.

Supplemental Reading

Bush, M.; Wildt, D. E.; Kennedy, S.; and Seager, S. W. J. 1978. Laparoscopy in zoological medicine. *JAVMA 173:* 173:1081-1087.

Czekala, N. M., and Lasley, B. L. 1977. A technical note on sex determination in monomorphic birds using faecal steroid analysis. *Inter. Zoo Yearbook* 17:209-211.

Harrison, G. J. 1978. Endoscopic examination of avian gonadal tissue. *Vet Med. Small Animal Clinics* 73:479-484.

McIlwaith, C. W., and Fessler, J. F. 1978. Arthroscopy in the diagnosis of equine joint disease. *JAVMA* 172:263-268.

Satterfield, W. C. 1980. Diagnostic laparoscopy in birds. In *Current Veterinary Therapy VII*, ed. R. W. Kirk. Philadelphia: W. B. Saunders Co.

Laparoscope with attachment for needle biopsy. The biopsy needle enters a special side port of the cannula

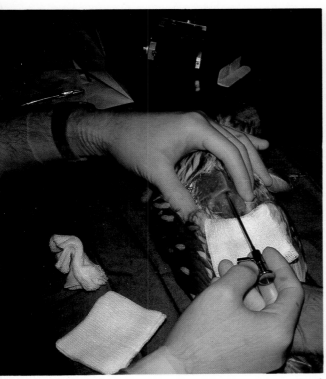
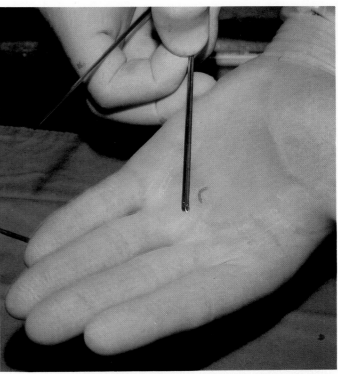

An immature night heron placed on its back for diagnostic liver biopsy to test for avian tuberculosis (above, left). The small piece of tissue in the palm is the sample taken from the liver (above, right). Placement of a single cat-gut suture in the skin of the night heron after biopsy (below).

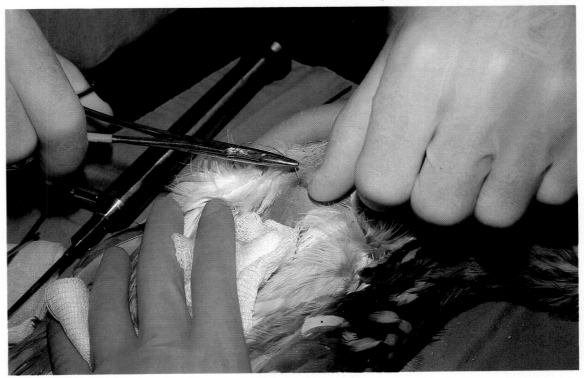